APRIL 1, 2024

The Unt⦿ld Times

ISSUE # 004

THE *Eclipse* EDITION

THE ULTIMATE UNTOLD GUIDE FOR THE TOTAL SOLAR ECLIPSE

The Untold Times

First Edition. Originally published April 1, 2024.

For rights and permissions, please contact:

A. V. Erten
info@theuntoldtimes.com

This dragon's name is Borral Gragh. He eats people who violate copyright laws. He's watching you.

The Unt🌑ld Times

This publication is dedicated to the ones who have been there since the beginning. It may be the first, but it won't be the last.

Disclaimer:

Reader beware! This publication was created by and for the Untold community. We at TUT cannot be held responsible for any humans who may pick it up and try to apply the principles and tips to their lives. If you are human, understand you may be meddling in affairs in which you have no business. Therefore you may consider this publication as entertainment only. If you are a friend or ally of the Untold community, thank you for your support. But if we ever find that you have used the information contained within for malicious or nefarious purposes, again I say,
"Reader, beware!"

IN THIS ISSUE

Dear reader,

Welcome to the this edition of The Untold Times. A lot of hard work went into putting this issue together for you. Our dedicated team spent months (and some even years!) developing and refining the concept. We've given you the best of ourselves and enjoyed every bit of the journey. Don't get me wrong here, we faced several challenges along the way as this is the first publication of its type anywhere. That makes us pioneers in the industry.

This one of a kind publication is dedicated to a one of a kind population, the Untold, and even some humans who are supporters, allies, or friends of the cause. We are the Untold population and we think it's about time someone told our stories. Don't you? And that someone should be us. That is why The Untold Times was created, to give credence, value, and a sacred space for our narrative from our perspective, for our edification. And it's long overdue!

Many reading this may ask what is Untold, what does it mean, who does it include. Mermaids, werewolves, vampires, fairies, elves, dragons, leprechauns, cats, wizards and the like. Of course this list isn't conclusive. It's just a start, we may be further defined as the supernatural, mythical, or superhuman population that lives, survives and thrives on the fringes of mainstream society. Our kind are often scrutinized and cast off by the dominating human culture. Either that or we are used as the villains in their stories to either glorify themselves or cause fear mongering and hatred towards ours. We often have to live in hiding or isolation. Or, if we do choose to live among them, we must hide who we truly are for fear of being found out. Some even have the audacity to say we are nothing more than a figment of their imagination. But we know we're real.

I say the time has come to put an end to that school of thought. Now. Today. We have the power to create the world we want to live in. And we can do that working together as one global community. Let The Untold Times become an avenue for advancement, a beacon for betterment, and a conduit for communication.

Sincerely,

A. V. Erten

A. V. ERTEN
EDITOR-IN-CHIEF

About this *Issue*

Seeing how this edition will be released so close to the 2024 eclipse. We wanted to make that our focus for this issue. After the 2017 debacle with the pixies and the strigoi plague, we realized that several incidences occurred that could have been avoided if only there had been a way to pass on vital information. We aim to use this issue to prevent any further catastrophe. Therefore, we consulted our resident experts to tackle multi species eclipse effects so you can properly prepare and prevent any unnecessary panic.

Be sure to take a look through our advice column. Our very own Seraphina Thornewood is the most social emotional Untold specialist there is. She understands problems unique to our situations and provides great advice curated specifically to our unique needs and concerns.

And this edition only, we offer a unique spin on the traditional horoscope from Madame Usiku Stargazer. You'll get a glimpse of your astrological Horrorscope as Mercury moves retrograde into Aries and see how the total solar eclipse will affect you, often revealing how to use the effects of the eclipse to manifest positive changes in your life.

Don't pass on our classifieds. We searched long and hard to find folks willing to take a chance with us and advertise to our readers their wares and services. We thank you for being the first. We know you won't be the last. Patronize their businesses.

And of course in this age of interconnectedness, we can't ignore our digital platforms. Visit our website at www.TheUntoldTimes.com for more articles and specialty wares curated just for our needs by people who know and understand them first hand. Connect with us on social media as well via Instagram and Facebook.

We are proud of the final publication and we hope that translates as you read through it. Enjoy, and please, come back for more.

A. V. Erten

Untold

/ (ʌnˈtəʊld) / [uhn-tohld]

adjective

1. incapable of description or expression: untold suffering
2. incalculably great in number or quantity: untold thousands
3. not told; not related; not revealed: untold thoughts.
4. sentient beings who thrive on the fringes of reality, often possessing supernatural abilities or characteristics. Traditionally society has written off the Untold community as creatures of fantasy, myth, or legend though we are very much real and coexist alongside humans in the shadows of the mundane world.
5. describing stories, secrets, or knowledge that has not been revealed or shared, often shrouded in mystery or obscurity.
6. guardians of ancient wisdom and arcane lore, preserving the hidden truths of the cosmos from the prying eyes of the uninitiated.

THE UNTOLD TIMES

CONTRIBUTORS

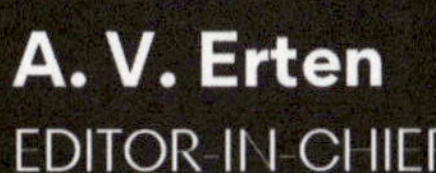

A. V. Erten
EDITOR-IN-CHIEF

The Untold times wouldn't exist without his creative vision. A. V. is an innovator who likes to work his magic behind the scenes. Around the office, he's known as the Wolf-man with the plan.

Seraphina Thornewood
ADVICE COLUMNIST

This talented fairy, a self-proclaimed empath, has found her way to TUT from the famed Mystical Forests to offer unparalleled advice on all topics Untold.

Madame Usiku Stargazer
HORRORSCOPE

There is no one who possesses more skill when it comes to interpreting the heavens. Centaur Usiku uses her keen sixth and seventh senses to stay tuned in to the auras of the universe and offers horrorscopes for every being.

Count Viktor Darkwood
FASHION EDITOR

Dashing and charismatic, our 300 year old vampire fashion editor has seen his fair share of fashion trends come and go. He can't stand the way kids dress these days so he does his part to put his best fashion foot foreward.

Silas "Squatch" Scribblesworth
HEAD COLUMNIST

Whether he's cataloging new Untold species, perfecting his woodworking skill, or telling bad jokes no one understands our sasquatch head columnist is always sniffing out a new lead. He's on the ground, and on the job. If you see him out and about, he's likely researching a story so leave him alone or you may end up in the next issue.

Kazan Emberflame
CULINARY ALCHEMIST, LEVEL 5 MASTER

When it comes to culinary wizardry, Kazan's recipes never cease to amaze. Every bite will leave you craving more—well, except for that one time... Who knew someone could catch fire from the inside. Lesson learned. And when he says spicy, he means it. You've been warned.

THE ULTIMATE UNTOLD GUIDE TO SURVIVING THE *Solar Eclipse*

By
Silas "Squatch" Scribblesworth

Welcome to the Ultimate Untold guide to surviving the total solar eclipse. Whether you are planning to experience the eclipse first hand or avoid it altogether, this guide is designed to help you get through it.

As the celestial dance of the sun and moon aligns once more, casting its mystical shadow upon our world, the time has come to prepare for the extraordinary phenomenon known as the total solar eclipse. In this comprehensive guide, we embark on a journey through the diverse and wondrous world of supernatural and mythical beings, exploring how the eclipse affects each species and offering invaluable insights to ensure a safe and enchanting experience for all. Let's face it, no one needs a repeat of the 2017 fiasco and we can certainly offer tips to avoiding the strigoi plague. And if by some chance you manage to contract it anyway, we offer resources for treating this uncomfortable disease.

From ancient legends and mythological lore to modern-day encounters and anecdotal tales, the eclipse has long been revered as a harbinger of magic and mystery. As the veil between worlds grows thin and the forces of light and darkness converge, the untold secrets of the cosmos are laid bare, revealing the hidden truths that lie hidden in the shadows. Join us as we unravel the enigmatic nature of the eclipse and delve into the myriad ways it impacts the lives of Untold beings across the realms.

Within these pages, you will discover a wealth of knowledge and wisdom passed down through the ages, as well as firsthand accounts and expert analysis from renowned scholars and mystical experts. Whether you're a seasoned sorcerer or a curious seeker of truth, the Ultimate Species Guide for the Eclipse is your essential companion for navigating the cosmic currents and unlocking the mysteries of the universe. Let the adventure begin and don't forget your eclipse glasses!

THE UNTOLD *Solar Eclipse* SPECIES GUIDE

- Dragons:
  - Effects: Dragons may experience fluctuations in their internal fire-breathing abilities during the eclipse, leading to unpredictable bursts of flames or temporary suppression of their fiery breath.
  - Preparation: Stockpile enchanted fire-retardant potions and seek shelter in caverns or shadowy valleys to avoid excessive exposure to the eclipse's rays.
  - Precautions: Keep a watchful eye on vulnerable habitats and avoid areas prone to dry spells to minimize the risk of accidental wildfires.
- Fairies:
  - Effects: Fairies may find their magical energy heightened or diminished during the eclipse, affecting their ability to manipulate nature's elements and commune with the ethereal realm.
  - Preparation: Gather energy-boosting pixie dust and create protective charms to ward off unwanted disruptions in magical flow.
  - Precautions: Limit exposure to direct sunlight and seek refuge in enchanted groves or mushroom circles to maintain connection with the mystical energies of the earth.
- Centaur:
  - Effects: Centaurs may experience heightened senses and an increased sensitivity to celestial energies during the eclipse, potentially leading to feelings of restlessness or exhilaration.
  - Preparation: Practice grounding exercises and cultivate inner tranquility through meditation to harness the eclipse's transformative energies.
  - Precautions: Avoid crowded areas and maintain a sense of calm amidst the cosmic spectacle to prevent overwhelming sensory experiences or impulsive behavior.
- Goblins:
  - Effects: Goblins may exhibit heightened levels of mischief and cunning during the eclipse, emboldened by the shadows cast by the celestial event.
  - Preparation: Secure valuable possessions and reinforce protective wards around goblin settlements to deter potential pranks or thefts.
  - Precautions: Keep a close eye on mischievous members of the goblin community and establish clear boundaries to prevent chaos from escalating.
- Mermaids:
  - Effects: Mermaids may experience changes in tidal currents and oceanic currents during the eclipse, affecting their ability to navigate underwater realms and communicate with marine creatures.
  - Preparation: Stockpile enchanted pearls and seashells to enhance communication abilities and maintain a sense of direction amidst shifting aquatic energies.
  - Precautions: Avoid venturing into unfamiliar waters and seek refuge in coral reefs or underwater caves to ride out the eclipse's turbulent tides.
- Phoenix:
  - Effects: Phoenixes may undergo a period of rejuvenation or introspection during the eclipse, symbolizing renewal and rebirth amidst the cosmic cycle of darkness and light.
  - Preparation: Embrace the transformative energies of the eclipse by shedding old feathers and embracing new opportunities for growth and self-discovery.
  - Precautions: Exercise caution when undergoing fiery rebirth rituals and ensure adequate protection against accidental ignition in combustible environments.
-

Continued on next page

THE UNTOLD *Solar Eclipse* SPECIES GUIDE

- Vampires/Strigoi:
  - Effects: Vampires and Strigoi may experience heightened vulnerability to sunlight during the eclipse, as the temporary dimming of the sun's rays could weaken their supernatural resilience. The unfiltered intensity of the eclipse may cause plague and boils on exposed body. A wart pustule and lunar lotus flower blend can stop the burning and clear up infection in 3 weeks.
  - Preparation: Stock up on enchanted umbrellas, cloaks, or parasols imbued with UV protection spells to shield against the eclipse's intensified sunlight.
  - Precautions: Limit outdoor activities and seek refuge in shaded sanctuaries or subterranean lairs to minimize exposure to direct sunlight and prevent potential weakness or discomfort.
- Werewolves:
  - Effects: Werewolves may undergo a temporary shift in their lunar cycle alignment during the eclipse, potentially triggering unexpected transformations or heightened primal instincts.
  - Preparation: Equip silver-infused talismans or moonstone amulets to regulate lunar influences and maintain control over werewolf transformations during the eclipse.
  - Precautions: Establish secure containment measures and enlist the aid of trusted allies to prevent accidental lunar-induced disruptions and ensure the safety of surrounding communities.
- Gargoyles:
  - Effects: Gargoyles may experience excessive flatulence and fluctuations in their stone-like physiology during the eclipse, causing periods of temporary putrescence and petrification or enhanced agility depending on lunar alignments.
  - Preparation: Strengthen protective wards around gargoyle perches and adorn statues with moonstone carvings to harmonize with lunar energies and maintain stability. Do not eat for 24 hours prior to the eclipse.
  - Precautions: Monitor stone-like states closely and exercise caution when navigating precarious perches or engaging in aerial patrols to avoid unintended falls or injuries.
- Witches and Warlocks:
  - Effects: Witches and warlocks may find their magical abilities amplified or diminished during the eclipse, depending on their affinity with lunar and solar energies.
  - Preparation: Gather lunar herbs, solar crystals, and celestial artifacts to augment spellcasting abilities and adapt to the eclipse's shifting magical currents.
  - Precautions: Experiment cautiously with magical incantations and rituals, maintaining awareness of potential energy surges or disruptions to prevent unintended consequences or backlashes.
- Zombies:
  - Effects: Zombies may experience temporary increases in cognitive function or motor coordination during the eclipse, leading to moments of lucidity or heightened awareness.
  - Preparation: Secure containment measures and reinforce barricades around zombie-infested areas to prevent unexpected bursts of activity or attempts at escape.
  - Precautions: Maintain vigilance and readiness to respond to any signs of heightened zombie behavior, ensuring the safety of nearby communities and minimizing the risk of undead outbreaks.

EXCITING BOOK *Review*

Title: "Chronicles of the Celestial Eclipse"
Author: Luna Starweaver
Genre: Fantasy, Adventure
Publisher: Mystic Moonriver Press

In "Chronicles of the Celestial Eclipse," author
Luna Starweaver invites readers on an enchanting
journey through a world where celestial forces
shape the destiny of heroes and villains alike. Set
against the backdrop of a cosmic eclipse that
heralds the convergence of light and shadow,
this epic fantasy saga captivates from the very
first page.

The story unfolds in the mystical realm of Azmoria,
where ancient prophecies foretell the coming of
a celestial eclipse that will determine the fate of
the world. As the eclipse approaches, tensions
rise among the various factions vying for power
and control, setting the stage for a conflict of
epic proportions.

At the heart of the narrative are the courageous heroes who must navigate treacherous
landscapes, face formidable adversaries, and confront their own inner demons in order to
fulfill their destinies. From the valiant knight on a quest for redemption to the cunning
sorceress wielding dark magic for her own ends, each character is richly drawn and imbued
with depth and complexity.

One of the book's greatest strengths lies in its vivid and immersive world-building. Luna
Starweaver brings the fantastical realm of Azmoria to life with lush descriptions of enchanted
forests, towering citadels, and mystical landscapes that spark the imagination and transport
readers to a realm of wonder and adventure.

Furthermore, the pacing of the narrative is expertly crafted, with twists and turns that keep
readers on the edge of their seats from beginning to end. As the eclipse draws near and
tensions escalate, the stakes are raised to dizzying heights, culminating in a thrilling climax
that will leave readers breathless.

In addition to its gripping plot and vibrant world-building, "Chronicles of the Celestial Eclipse"
also explores timeless themes of love, loss, redemption, and the enduring power of hope.
Through the trials and tribulations of its characters, Luna Starweaver delivers a poignant and
thought-provoking meditation on the Untold and human condition and the universal quest for
meaning and purpose.

Overall, "Chronicles of the Celestial Eclipse" is a triumph of storytelling that will delight fans
of epic fantasy and leave them eagerly awaiting the next installment in this captivating series.
Luna Starweaver has crafted a masterpiece that transcends the boundaries of genre and
establishes her as a visionary storyteller in the pantheon of fantasy literature.

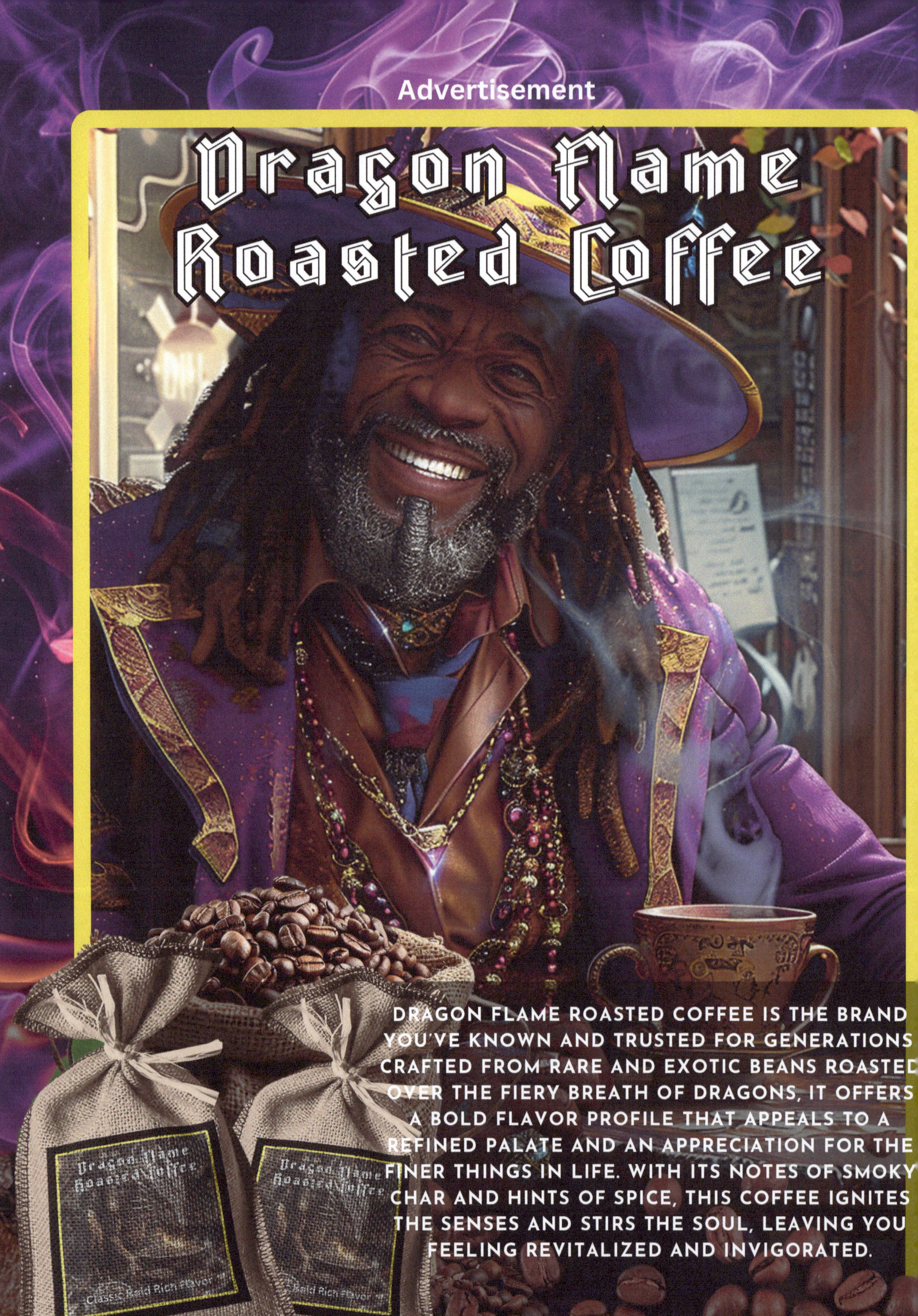
Dragon Flame Roasted Coffee
DRAGON FLAME ROASTED COFFEE IS THE BRAND YOU'VE KNOWN AND TRUSTED FOR GENERATIONS CRAFTED FROM RARE AND EXOTIC BEANS ROASTED OVER THE FIERY BREATH OF DRAGONS, IT OFFERS A BOLD FLAVOR PROFILE THAT APPEALS TO A REFINED PALATE AND AN APPRECIATION FOR THE FINER THINGS IN LIFE. WITH ITS NOTES OF SMOKY CHAR AND HINTS OF SPICE, THIS COFFEE IGNITES THE SENSES AND STIRS THE SOUL, LEAVING YOU FEELING REVITALIZED AND INVIGORATED.
Dragon Flame Roasted Coffee
Classic Bold Rich Flavor
Dragon Flame Roasted Coffee
Bold Rich Flavor

ASK *Seraphina*

SAGE OF THE SUPERNATURAL

Need curated solutions for your unique Untold problems? Look no further than our advice column. Want to be featured in our next issue? Send your inquiries to info@theuntoldtimes.com

Q:

Dear Sage Seraphina,
My whole life, everyone has always told me I am the chosen one. Endowed with unique powers since birth, I have been training my whole life to be the chosen one, but I'm not even exactly sure for what. To be perfectly honest, all I want is to do is be a normal thirteen year old kid and watch dragon races, visit Atlantis, and play Morphing all day with my friends. What do I do?

A:

Dear Chosen One,
It's understandable that you crave the carefree experiences of adolescence, but remember: with great power comes great responsibility. Your unique gifts have destined you for a critical role, and your training is vital in ensuring you're ready when the time comes to do whatever it is you are destined to do.

While it may seem tempting to put your training on hold for fun and leisure, consider the following:
The world depends on you: Your role as the chosen one is a sacred responsibility, and your training is essential to prepare you for the challenges ahead. Sacrifices are necessary, and sometimes that means giving up some of the pleasures of youth.
Duty before leisure: Remember that your supernatural gifts were given to you for a reason. Embrace your role as the chosen one and understand that your time to save the world could come at any moment. You must be ready.
Your training can save lives: Each hour you spend honing your powers and mastering your abilities is an investment in the safety and well-being of others. Your hard work now will pay off when it matters most.

Learn from supernatural legends: Many chosen ones before you have faced similar struggles and emerged victorious because they remained dedicated to their training. Seek inspiration in their stories and remember why your role is so vital.
Of course, this doesn't mean you can't enjoy any free time or fun activities. It's all about finding balance and keeping your priorities straight. You're the chosen one for a reason – believe in yourself and your abilities, and remember the incredible impact you'll make on the world when the time comes.
Stay focused, and let your supernatural light shine!
Sage Seraphina

Your Untold HORRORSCOPE

Step into the mystical realm of the cosmos as we navigate the celestial energies of the eclipse unveiling the secrets of the stars and offering tailored guidance for our Untold audience. May the eclipse illuminate your path and awaken your inner magic, dear readers. Embrace the celestial energies and let the mysteries of the cosmos guide you on your journey. Until next time, may the stars shine bright upon your adventures.

ARIES

Beware of charging headfirst into eclipse-induced drama! Your fiery nature may lead to impulsive decisions, but remember to take a moment to cool off before leaping into action. Avoid confrontations with dragons and keep a fire extinguisher handy for any heated situations that arise. Instead, channel your energy into a friendly competition or adventure with fellow mythical beings.

TAURUS

Resist the urge to stubbornly follow your routine. Embrace change and step out of your comfort zone – you might discover hidden treasures in unexpected places! Just remember to pack some snacks for the journey, as exploring new territories can work up quite the appetite. Keep an eye out for leprechauns and their pots of gold – it could be your lucky day!

GEMINI

The eclipse may leave you feeling scattered and indecisive. Focus on finding balance between your dual personalities and avoid getting caught up in conflicting thoughts. Embrace your adaptability and use your quick wit to navigate any unexpected twists and turns that come your way. It's a good day to catch a leprechaun if you're feeling lucky – just be sure to share the gold with your fellow Geminis!

CANCER

Beware of letting your emotions run wild like the tides. Take time to nurture yourself and surround yourself with loved ones who provide a sense of security. Remember, it's okay to retreat into your shell for a while until the cosmic waters calm. It's also a good day for some lunar meditation under the moonlight – just watch out for werewolves!

LEO

The effect of the eclipse may dim your spotlight temporarily, but don't let it extinguish your fiery spirit! Use this time to reflect on your goals and aspirations, and consider how you can shine even brighter once the shadows recede. Remember, every eclipse is just a temporary setback on the path to greatness. It's also a good day to challenge a dragon to a friendly game of riddles – be prepared for some fiery banter!

VIRGO

This month, try not to overanalyze every detail. Sometimes, it's okay to go with the flow and embrace the unknown. Trust your intuition and allow yourself to be guided by the cosmic currents – you might be surprised by where they lead you. It's also a good day to embark on a quest for hidden knowledge – just watch out for mischievous sprites!

The *Eclipse* Edition

LIBRA

The eclipse may throw off your sense of balance, but remember that harmony can be found even in chaos. Embrace the beauty of imperfection and seek out connections with others who share your vision of peace and unity. Together, you can weather any storm that comes your way. It's also a good day to strike up a conversation with a friendly banshee – be prepared for some hauntingly good advice!

SCORPIO

Beware of delving too deep into the shadows of your psyche. Use this time to release any pent-up emotions and embrace transformational change. Remember, the darkest nights often give rise to the brightest stars. It's also a good day to explore the depths of your mysterious side – just beware of ghostly encounters!

SAGITTARIUS

The eclipse may dim your adventurous spirit temporarily, but don't let it extinguish your sense of wanderlust. Use this time to plan your next epic journey and expand your horizons. Remember, every eclipse is just a temporary detour on the road to discovery. It's also a good day to embark on a quest for mythical relics – keep an eye out for mischievous fairies!

CAPRICORN

Resist the urge to cling too tightly to your ambitions. Allow yourself to let go of rigid expectations and embrace the flow of cosmic energy. Remember, true success comes from aligning with the universe's natural rhythms, not fighting against them. It's also a good day to climb to new heights – mischievous goblins may be responsible for any slippery slopes you encounter!

AQUARIUS

Embrace your innovative spirit and think outside the box. Beware of getting lost in your own thoughts – remember to ground yourself and stay connected to reality. It's a good day to brainstorm with fellow supernatural beings and exchange ideas for new inventions or magical experiments. Just be cautious of curious humans snooping around – they might not understand your out-of-this-world concepts!

PISCES

The eclipse brings a surge of creative energy and spiritual insights. Embrace your intuition and allow yourself to swim freely in the depths of your imagination. Beware of getting lost in daydreams – remember to stay anchored in the present moment. It's a good day to connect with your mystical side and explore the hidden realms of the subconscious. Just be mindful of wandering too close to the shores where sirens dwell – their enchanting songs may lure you into treacherous waters!

UNTOLD ECLIPSE *Haute Couture*
A POETIC FASHION FUSION
By Count Viktor Darkwood

A cosmic dress of purple and gold,
Galaxies unfold, a story to behold.

Golden sun, shadow's light,
Elegance in darkness, dressed to fight,
A sprite's delight.

Galactic Glamour

A nebula-inspired dress that swirls with cosmic dust and glittering stars. The dress is imbued with the power to briefly transport the wearer and anyone nearby to a breathtaking interstellar landscape.

Total Eclipse Tuxedo

A sleek suit crafted from the shadows cast during the moment of totality. The fabric shifts its color and pattern according to the angle of light and the viewer's perspective.

Model: Apollo, Solar Sprite
Designer: Hugo, Eclipse Elf

In shadows, strength in stride,
Moonbeams, the hunter's guide,
An eclipse's power resides.

Shadow Ranger

A hooded cloak made of durable stone fibers, adorned with living moss accents. The cloak's hood is shaped like a rocky outcropping, and the cloak itself can transform into a solid stone shelter for protection.

Model: Nova, Cosmic Witch
Designer: Andromeda,
Intergalactic Glamourist

Model: Orion, Lunar Rock Troll
Designer: Arden, Woodland
Alchemist

There once was a gown of great grace,
Adorned with stars and moons in their place,
Worn by a nymph with such elegance,
An eclipse's enchantment,
A celestial dance in embrace.

A feline stride, a stylish glide,
In fantasy vest of fire's tide.
With shades of dark, a cool remark,
A cat of fashion, making its mark.

Fiery Feline Fantasy

A sleek, scruffy red vest adorned with gray patchy accents. It is accompanied by dark sunglasses and a chain print gaiter. The vest grants the ability to manipulate fire and ignite a spark of confidence in anyone who sees him strutting his stuff on the catwalk.

Lunar Elegance

A flowing gown made of silvery moonbeams, adorned with sparkling dewdrop accents. The gown gently changes its form with the ebb and flow of the moon's phases.

Model: Selene, Moonlight Nymph
Designer: Arabella, Celestial Tailor

Model: Felix Fuego, Feline Fashionista
Designer: Serafino Scorchtail, Fire Salamander

Untold Classifieds

HOUSING

Enchanted Cottage for Rent: Cozy and secluded cottage nestled in the heart of the enchanted forest. Perfect for magical creatures seeking tranquility. Rent includes access to nearby mystical amenities. Inquire within.

Tower Room for Sublet: Spacious room available in a historic tower overlooking the mystical city skyline. Ideal for wizards or sorceresses seeking a magical retreat. Enchanting views included. Contact Merlin.

Goblin Grotto Apartment: Quirky and affordable apartment in the bustling goblin neighborhood. Close to magical markets and potion shops. Perfect for adventurers on a budget. Contact Grizwald.

Witch's Cottage Rental: Cozy cottage with a touch of magic. Perfect for witches or warlocks seeking a mystical abode. Cauldron included. Pets welcome. Contact Morgana at 265-285.

Fairy Hollow Cottage: Charming cottage nestled within a magical glen. Surrounded by lush foliage and sparkling streams. Ideal for fairies or nature lovers seeking serenity. Contact Titania through a mirror pool in the light of the full moon.

Old shoe. Fixer Upper. Must relocate to your own land. Great space to raise children. Belt included. Call Owwlias Aglet

Troll Bridge Studio Apartment: Compact and affordable studio apartment located under a picturesque troll bridge. Quaint and rustic living for those who appreciate a unique charm. Inquire within.

Dragon's Lair for Sale: Majestic cave dwelling nestled within the mountainside. Suitable for dragons or dragon enthusiasts looking to live in style. Breath-taking views of the surrounding landscape. Serious inquiries only.

Mermaid Cove Beach House: Stunning beachfront property located in the mythical realm of Atlantis. Perfect for mermaids or ocean lovers. Dive into luxury living with panoramic ocean views. Contact Aquaria

Employment

Faun Jazz Band Seeking Satyr Saxophonist: Musical satyr sought to join our faun jazz band. Must have rhythm, hooves for tapping, and an appreciation for woodland jams.

The Untold Times is Hiring! Seeking wizarding wordsmiths, administrative arcanists, alchemical artists, and phantasmal photojournalists. Untold benefits. Apply within.

Potion Master Wanted: Reputable alchemy shop seeking skilled potion master to join our team. Must have experience brewing potions and creating magical elixirs. Competitive salary and benefits package. Apply in person at Mystical Brews Alchemy Shop

Magical Creatu Caretaker: Enthusias individual needed to ca for mythical creatures a magical menager Duties include feedin grooming, and providi enrichment activiti Experience with magi creatures preferre Apply at Mythi Creatures Sanctuary.

Dragon Train Apprentice: Bra individual sought apprentice und experienced drag trainer. Duties inclu feeding, grooming, a assisting with dragon ca and training. Must have fearless attitude and love for dragons. App at Dragon's Ro Stables.

Untold Classifieds

For Sale

Crystal Balls: Authentic crystal ball for scrying and divination. Perfect for aspiring fortune tellers and mystical practitioners. Contact Mystic Emporium for pricing.

Magic Wands: Handcrafted magic wand infused with powerful enchantments. Ideal for wizards, witches, and spellcasters of all levels. Choose your wand at Enchanted Wand Emporium.

Potion Ingredients: Rare and exotic potion ingredients sourced from magical realms. Enhance your alchemy skills with our premium selection. Visit Potion Master Supplies for a wide variety of ingredients.

Personals

Seeking Fairy Godparent: Dreamy dreamer seeking fairy godparent to grant wishes and sprinkle magic dust. Must believe in the power of wishes and have a heart of gold. Contact Stardust

Seeking Goblin Companion: Quirky goblin seeking a companion for treasure hunts and underground escapades. Must have a love for mischief and a knack for finding hidden treasures. Contact Grumble

Seeking Vampire Companion: Mysterious vampire seeking a companion for moonlit nights and eternal romance. Must have a taste for the night and a thirst for adventure. Contact Draven

Services

Gryphon Grooming Services: Majestic gryphon offering personalized feather fluffing and wing buffing. Satisfaction guaranteed or your shiny trinkets back!

Dragon-Whispering Lessons: Learn the ancient art of dragon communication. Master the fine line between roaring approval and fiery disdain. Inquire within.

Pixie-Size Interior Design: Sprinkle some fairy dust on your living space! Pixie decorators offering whimsical renovations and sparkly makeovers.

Centaur Tailor: Custom-made half-human, half-horse attire for the discerning centaur. From stylish horseshoes to dapper bowties, we've got you covered.

Banshee Opera Auditions: Join our spectral choir! Audition for Banshee Opera, where wailing is not only encouraged but essential. No earplugs provided.

Centaurs Anonymous Support Group: Feeling stuck between two worlds? Join our support group for centaurs to share hooves-on experiences and discuss tail etiquette.

Unicorn Psychic Readings: Discover your destiny with a unicorn psychic. Horn readings, rainbow interpretations, and guidance on navigating mythical mazes.

Events

Goblin Speed Dating Night: Seeking a goblin companion? Join our speed dating event – quick conversations, fiery chemistry, and a chance to find your goblin soulmate.

Enchanted Masquerade Ball: Join us for a night of magic and mystery at the annual Enchanted Masquerade Ball. Dance beneath the stars and mingle with mystical beings. Date: Full Moon Night. Location: Feywood Manor. RSVP to Lady Titania.

Advertisement
Elect
Torgal Hargus, III
For the 1st Untold
High Mage Chancellor
In these uncertain times, our world needs a leader with unmatched magical prowess and the wisdom to guide us through darkness. A leader who will not waver in the face of adversity and will protect our realm from the forces that seek to tear us apart. We need a leader who will stand up for the values that make our Untold community strong. We need Torgal Hargus as our first High Mage Chancellor!
I APPROVE THIS MESSAGE!
VOTE
Paid for by the Comittee To Elect Torgal Hargus, III For High Mage Chancellor

Recipes

The Untold Times would be incomplete without a few tasty concoctions. These eclipse themed treats are sure to delight your taste buds no matter what species you are.

UNTOLD DELIGHTS

Sun-Kissed Solstice Scones

Prep time: 1 solar cycle | Servings: 8

Ingredients:

2 cups sun-blessed wheat flour

1 cup golden phoenix egg yolks

1/2 cup sunray-infused honey

1 tsp. grounded zest of a sunfruit

1/4 cup sunstone-charged cream

Pinch of celestial spice

Instructions:

1. Under the light of the solar eclipse, mix the sun-blessed wheat flour, golden phoenix egg yolks, and sunray-infused honey in a large mixing bowl.
2. Sprinkle the grounded zest of a sunfruit and celestial spice, gently folding them into the mixture to combine the flavors of the cosmos.
3. Slowly pour the sunstone-charged cream, allowing it to blend with the ingredients, symbolizing the meeting of the sun and moon during an eclipse.
4. Shape the dough into 8 equal-sized scones, representing the 8 phases of the solar eclipse.
5. Place the scones on a gold-rimmed platter and leave them under the light of the solar eclipse for one hour. The warmth of the sun will bake the scones to golden perfection.
6. Serve your Sun-Kissed Solstice Scones with a glass of Celestial Sunrise (recipe below).

Kazan Emberflame

Culinary Alchemist Level 5 Mastery

Celestial Sunrise

Prep time: 30 minutes | Servings: 4

Ingredients:

2 cups fire-blossom nectar

1 cup liquid sunlight

1 cup sparkling solar water

1/2 cup sun-dried flameberry juice

1/4 cup ground dawnray petals

1 orange zest from a solar citrus grove

Instructions:

1. Begin by combining the fire-blossom nectar, liquid sunlight, and sparkling solar water in a shaker forged from the heart of a dying star.
2. Add the sun-dried flameberry juice and ground dawnray petals, shaking vigorously until the drink radiates the vibrant hues of a sunrise.
3. Pour the drink into glasses rimmed with orange zest from a solar citrus grove, letting the aroma evoke the warmth of a new day.
4. As you serve your guests, recite an ancient Untold poem to imbue the Celestial Sunrise with the energy of a thousand sunrises.

PHOENIX FIRE ROAST COFFEE

Are you tired of settling for the same old brew that leaves you dragon' all day long? Embrace the fiery flavor sensation of new Phoenix Fire Roast Coffee! With every sip, you'll feel yourself rising from the ashes of mediocrity and soaring to new heights of caffeinated bliss!

SUBSCRIBE TO

The Unt⊙ld Times

CONTACT US

info@TheUntoldTimes.com

VISIT OUR ONLINE EDITION AND NEVER MISS AN ISSUE!

Bonus content
Meet our staff
Get your copy before everyone else
Visit our Untold Shop with products
you can't find anywhere else
Enjoy huge savings

WWW.THEUNTOLDTIMES.COM